TEAMS OF THE NFC

SCHOLASTIC INC.

NEW YORK   TORONTO   LONDON   AUCKLAND

SYDNEY   MEXICO CITY   NEW DELHI   HONG KONG

Photo Credits

Page 4: © David J. Phillip/Associated Press; Page 5 (top) © Gene J. Puskar/Associated Press, (bottom) © Bill Kostroun/Associated Press; Page 6: (top) © Dick Druckman/Associated Press, (bottom) © Rob Carr/Associated Press; Page 7: (top) © Matt Slocum/Associated Press, (bottom) © Brian Garfinkel/Associated Press; Page 8: (top) © David Drapkin/Associated Press, (bottom) © Evan Vucci/Associated Press; Page 9: © Bill Nichols/Associated Press; Page 10: (top) © Charles Rex Arbogast/Associated Press, (bottom) © Nam Y. Huh/Associated Press; Page 11: (top) © Paul Sancya/Associated Press, (bottom) © Tom DiPace/Associated Press; Page 12: © David Stluka/ Associated Press; Page 13: © Paul Spinelli/Associated Press; Page 14: © Paul Abell/Associated Press; Page 15: © Paul Abell/Associated Press; Page 16: (top) © Thomas E. Witte/Associated Press, (bottom) © Tom DiPace/ Associated Press; Page 17: © Paul Jasienski/Associated Press, (bottom) Mark J. Terrill/Associated Press; Page 18: © Tom DiPace/Associated Press; Page 19: © Greg Trott/Associated Press; Page 20: (bottom) © Paul Connors/ Associated Press, (bottom) © Tom Gannam/Associated Press; Page 21: © Jeff Roberson/Associated Press; Page 22: (top) © Greg Trott/Associated Press, (bottom) © Ben Liebenberg/Associated Press; Page 23: (top) © Greg Trott/Associated Press, (bottom) © Kevin Terrell/Associated Press

ISBN 978-0-545-34637-5

12 11 10 9 8 7 6 5 4 3 2 1   11 12 13 14 15/0

Printed in the U.S.A.   40

First printing, September 2011

The NFC

The National Football League (NFL) was formed in 1920 in an automobile showroom in Canton, Ohio. Several owners of professional teams got together and decided that they needed to be organized and to play under the same rules. So they formed a group they called the American Professional Football Association (APFA). The league played under that name in 1920 and 1921, and then was renamed the NFL in 1922.

For 40 years, the NFL was the undisputed king of football. Other leagues tried to compete with the NFL, but failed. Finally, in 1960, a new American Football League (AFL) took the field. That league succeeded, in large part because of a network television deal that kept its teams afloat financially. In 1966, the AFL and the NFL agreed that, beginning in 1970, they would join together to form an even bigger NFL.

When the two leagues got together, the larger NFL split into the American Football Conference (AFC) and the National Football Conference (NFC). The NFC consisted of 13 teams that already belonged in the NFL. Three more established NFL teams — the Baltimore (now Indianapolis) Colts, Cleveland Browns, and Pittsburgh Steelers — joined the 10 former AFL teams in the AFC.

The Dallas Cowboys, Los Angeles (now St. Louis) Rams, and Minnesota Vikings were the best teams of the NFC in the 1970s. In 1981, the San Francisco 49ers won their first Super Bowl. They began a remarkable stretch of 16 years in which NFC teams won the Super Bowl 15 times. Through Super Bowl XLV in the 2010 season, NFC teams won 24 Super Bowls; AFC teams won 21.

Among NFC teams, the Cowboys have played in the most Super Bowls, with eight. They have won five of them, tying the San Francisco 49ers for the most victories in the NFC. Nine of the sixteen NFC teams have won the Super Bowl. Detroit is the only NFC team that has never made it to the NFL's biggest game.

The Green Bay Packers won the Super Bowl for the fourth time in the 2010 season. Green Bay beat the AFC-champion Pittsburgh Steelers 31-25 in Super Bowl XLV at the Cowboys' home stadium in North Texas.

Super Bowl Victories by NFC Team:

Team	Wins	Team	Wins
Dallas Cowboys	5	Tampa Bay Buccaneers	1
San Francisco 49ers	5	Detroit Lions	0
Green Bay Packers	4	Philadelphia Eagles	0
New York Giants	3	Minnesota Vikings	0
Washington Redskins	3	Atlanta Falcons	0
Chicago Bears	1	Carolina Panthers	0
New Orleans Saints	1	Seattle Seahawks	0
St. Louis Rams	1	Arizona Cardinals	0

NFC East

Even though none of the NFC East teams were around when the NFL first began playing in 1920, each soon came along and left its mark.

For instance, the Giants played a major role in helping to stabilize the young league after they were founded in 1925. The Redskins began in 1932 under the direction of founder George Preston Marshall who proposed the idea of splitting the NFL into two divisions and creating an annual championship game. The Eagles started in 1933, and featured the league's top star in the late 1940s, when pro football was competing for national attention in the years following World War II. And when the Dallas Cowboys began playing in 1960, they were the first NFL team to embrace technology by using computers to evaluate players.

These teams aren't all about ancient history, though! They have been among the NFL's most successful in the Super Bowl era, too. Dallas was just the second NFL team (after the San Francisco 49ers) to win the Super Bowl five times. The Giants and Redskins each have won three Super Bowls. And while the Eagles haven't won a Super Bowl yet, they've reached the playoffs more than any other team in the division.

In 2010, in fact, Philadelphia won the NFC East crown for the fifth time since the division went to its current four-team format in 2002. (Before that, the Cardinals also played in the NFC East.) If history is any indication, though, you can expect the other NFC East teams to be back in the title chase again soon.

DALLAS COWBOYS

When it comes to the Dallas Cowboys, it seems as if every football fan in the country either really, really likes them — or really, really does not! Love 'em or hate 'em, though, there's no denying that the Cowboys are the one of the most successful franchises in league history.

Although the Cowboys did not begin playing until 1960, their impressive 30 seasons in the playoffs equal the New York Giants. Dallas' eight Super Bowls equal the Pittsburgh Steelers for the most ever, and the Cowboys' five Super Bowl wins equal the second most. No other NFL team has come close to their 20 consecutive seasons with a winning record (from 1966 to 1985).

Some of football's biggest stars have worn a Cowboys' uniform, from quarterback Roger Staubach and defensive lineman Bob Lilly in the early days of the franchise to quarterback Troy Aikman and running back Emmitt Smith during the team's dynasty days in the 1990s. Those Cowboys won three Super Bowls in four seasons beginning in 1992. They haven't been back to the Super Bowl since beating Pittsburgh in the 1995 season, although they've been to the playoffs several times.

Tony Romo

Today's Stars

There's always a lot of star power in Dallas, where football is the king of sports. Quarterback Tony Romo is the brightest star. He's made the Pro Bowl three times. Miles Austin is one game-breaking wide receiver, while Dez Bryant (a rookie in 2010) looks like he might be another soon.

Miles Austin

A Prayer Answered

A desperation pass at the end of the first half or the game is known as a Hail Mary pass. That term originated with the Cowboys in 1975, when quarterback Roger Staubach threw a long touchdown pass in the final minute to beat the Vikings in a playoff game. "I threw it as far as I could and said a Hail Mary," Staubach said.

The way the story goes, the New York Giants came about by accident. In 1925, businessman Tim Mara was trying to invest in a famous heavyweight boxer when he found out he could place an NFL franchise in New York for $500. The rest, as they say, is history. The Giants made their debut that season and quickly became one of the cornerstone franchises in the league. Having a thriving team in New York was important to the NFL because it helped pro football gain national attention.

It helped, too, that the Giants were pretty good almost from the beginning — and most of the time since, too. New York has been to the playoffs 30 times, which equals the Dallas Cowboys for the most ever. The Giants have won 7 league championships; only Green Bay (12) and Chicago (9) have won more. Under head coach Bill Parcells, the Giants won Super Bowls XXI (1986 season) and XXV (1990 season). Their most recent Super Bowl win, under current coach Tom Coughlin, was game XLII (2007 season), when they ended New England's dream of a perfect season.

The Giants won 10 games in 2010 but missed out on the playoffs due to a tiebreaker. It was only the third time in Coughlin's seven seasons as coach that they didn't reach the postseason — so expect them back soon!

Derek Hagan

Hakeem Nicks

Today's Stars

Quarterback Eli Manning is more than just Colts quarterback Peyton Manning's little brother. Eli is a Super Bowl-winning, Super Bowl-MVP quarterback himself. Manning's top target is one of the fastest-rising stars among NFL receivers: Hakeem Nicks. On defense, Pro Bowl star Jason Tuck continues a tradition of great Giants' defensive ends.

6

PHILADELPHIA EAGLES

The bad news for Philadelphia Eagles fans is that it's been a very long time since their team has won a league championship — 50 years! The good news is that the team has been the best in the NFC since the 2000s began. The Eagles, in fact, have been to the playoffs more times (nine) than any other NFC team since the 2000 season. They won the NFC championship in the 2004 season before losing a close game to the Patriots in the Super Bowl.

The Eagles' franchise began in 1933. In the late 1940s, the Eagles had the best team (they won the championship in both 1948 and 1949) and one of the best players (Hall of Fame running back Steve Van Buren). The Eagles won another title in 1960 in Hall of Fame quarterback Norm Van Brocklin's last game. Quarterback Donovan McNabb and running back Brian Westbrook were the key players in several of the team's trips to the postseason in the 2000s.

All those trips to the playoffs haven't resulted in a Super Bowl victory — yet. But even as players such as McNabb and Westbrook have moved on, the Eagles keep right on winning. And that's very good news for Eagles' fans.

Michael Vick

Today's Stars

Head coach Andy Reid's Eagles are known for their speed and big-play ability. Quarterback Michael Vick has a strong arm, but he also can run as well as he throws. Wide receiver DeSean Jackson catches more long touchdown passes than just about anyone else in the game. He's a great punt returner, too. On defense, cornerback Asante Samuel has led the league in interceptions twice in his NFL career.

weather or Not

In sunshine or rain, snow or mud, the game goes on in the NFL. The Eagles have played in two of the most famous bad-weather games ever. In 1948, the Eagles won the "Snow Game" for the league title beating the Chicago Cardinals 7-0 on a field completely covered by snow. In 1988, the Eagles lost to the Bears 20-12 in the playoffs in the "Fog Bowl." It was so foggy in Chicago that day that the quarterbacks couldn't see receivers down the field!

DeSean Jackson

WASHINGTON REDSKINS

In the first year of the Redskins franchise, they were known as the Boston Braves. They became the Redskins in 1933 and moved to Washington in 1937. Owner George Preston Marshall was a showman who helped build his fan base in Washington by writing a fight song, starting a marching band, organizing halftime shows, and, eventually, televising games. He made Redskins games fun, win or lose. Most of the time, the Redskins won. With Sammy Baugh starring on both offense and defense, the team won the NFL championship its first season in Washington, and then again in 1942.

The Redskins' greatest success, though, came later under head coach Joe Gibbs. From 1982 to 1991, the Redskins won the Super Bowl three times. Gibbs' teams featured Pro Football Hall of Fame players such as running back John Riggins and cornerback Darrell Green. Mostly, though, it was known for a mammoth group of offensive linemen affectionately known as "The Hogs."

Young tackles Jammal Brown and Trent Williams try to help carry on the tradition of "The Hogs" on the current Redskins' team. But the Redskins have only had a couple of winning seasons since the 2000s began (they came when Gibbs returned to coach the team a second time). Mike Shanahan, who helped Denver win two Super Bowls in the 1990s, was brought in as the new head coach in 2010.

Andre Carter

DeAngelo Hall

Today's Stars

Head coach Mike Shanahan is known as an offensive mastermind, but the team he inherited has its biggest stars on the defensive side of the football. Linebacker Brian Orakpo was a first-round draft pick who has been in the league two years — and made the Pro Bowl two times. Cornerback DeAngelo Hall tied an NFL record last season when he intercepted four passes in a single game.

When you think of football, do you think of games played in the rain and the mud and the snow? Do you think of frozen tundras and wind-chill factors and old-time, smash-mouth defense? If you do, then the NFC North is the place for you.

The Chicago Bears, Detroit Lions, Green Bay Packers, and Minnesota Vikings play in the NFC North. No other NFL division packs as much history into it as this one. The Bears, Lions, and Packers have been around since the early days of the NFL, while the Vikings played their 50th season in 2010.

For a long time, too, these clubs have been among the NFL's most rough-and-tumble teams. In fact, when they used to play in the NFC Central Division, it commonly was called the "Black and Blue Division" — and that wasn't for any of the team's uniform colors!

In 2002, the teams of the NFC Central (minus the Tampa Bay Buccaneers) made up the newly formed NFC North which took on the "Black and Blue Division" nickname. And while things aren't quite the same as they used to be — the Lions and Vikings, for instance, play their home games indoors now instead of out in the elements — a rugged brand of football is still the way to the top in this division.

In 2010, the Bears won the NFC North and the Packers earned a playoff berth as a wild-card team. Both teams feature well-known stars on offense. But both teams also got as far as they did because of defenses that were stingy about giving up points. The Packers ranked second in the league in that category in 2010, and the Bears were fourth.

The Vikings missed the playoffs in 2010. They don't figure to stay on the sideline for long, though — Minnesota has made the playoffs more times than it hasn't in its 50-year history. The Lions, meanwhile, have been on the outside of the playoffs looking in since the 2000s began. But with the way they finished the 2010 season, that could change soon.

Tim Jennings (26) and Greg Jennings (85)

CHICAGO BEARS

Since the early days of the franchise, which actually began in Decatur, Illinois in 1920 before moving to Chicago in 1921, the Chicago Bears have been known as "The Monsters of the Midway." (The Midway is a famous stretch of parkland in Chicago.) There's a reason for the ferocious nickname. The Bears almost always have been known for their intimidating defenses. Even the names of some of the club's all-time greats — like Bronko Nagurski, Dan Fortmann, and Dick Butkus — are intimidating.

The Bears' history is more than just great defense, though. George Halas, who coached the team for 40 years and owned the club for more than that, was one of the most influential figures in pro football history. Gale Sayers, from the 1960s, and Walter Payton, from the 1970s and 1980s, are two of the most dynamic running backs ever.

The Bears have had more Hall of Famers than any other team. They have played in more history-shaping games than perhaps any other team. Their nine NFL championships are the second most in the league. Now, the current Bears are living up to the standard set by their ancestors. Chicago won the NFC North for the third time in 2010 and made the playoffs for the fourth time in 10 years.

Jay Cutler

Matt Forté

Today's Stars

Head coach Lovie Smith's current team keeps up the Bears' defensive tradition with star linebackers Lance Briggs and Brian Urlacher. But Chicago also features one of the best and most-balanced offenses the team ever has had. Quarterback Jay Cutler can move the ball through the air. Running back Matt Forté grinds out yards on the ground and is a good pass catcher, too. It's that combination of offense and defense that made the Bears the best in the NFC North in 2010.

DETROIT LIONS

You've got to back a long way to find a time when the Lions ruled the NFL. When you do, though, you'll see that they once were one of the proudest franchises in the league.

Detroit began its existence as the Portsmouth Spartans in 1930. Four years later, the team moved to Detroit and became the Lions. In 1935, the Lions won their first NFL championship. Later, in the 1950s, Detroit was an annual title contender. With Hall of Famers Bobby Layne (a quarterback) and Joe Schmidt (a linebacker) leading the way, the team won three NFL Championship Games — that was the Super Bowl before there was a Super Bowl — in a span of six seasons beginning in 1952.

After that, though, the Lions fell on hard times. In the 1990s, the team had some pretty good seasons, but never made the Super Bowl. In the 2000s, Detroit sunk lower than ever, and in 2008 hit rock bottom: The team lost every game. Now, though, things are looking up. Head coach Jim Schwartz, who took over in 2009, is a defensive specialist who has helped the Lions improve greatly on that side of the ball in just a short time. On offense, several young players figure to help make the Lions proud once again.

Matthew Stafford

Today's Stars

While the Lions haven't had much success in recent years, they're definitely a team on the rise. Young stars such as quarterback Matthew Stafford, running back Jahvid Best, and wide receiver Calvin Johnson give Detroit plenty of offense. And the arrival of lineman Ndamukong Suh has bolstered the defense. Suh made the Pro Bowl as a rookie in 2010. The Lions finished that season strong, and they expect to make big strides in 2011.

Ndamukong Suh

Catch Him If You Can!

The Lions' Barry Sanders was one of the most electrifying running backs in football history. At 5 feet 8 inches, Sanders was a little guy by NFL standards. But he had immensely strong legs and lightning-quick moves. Sanders would dart one way, and then another, and then spin around —leaving defensive players grasping at air! Sanders played in Detroit for 10 seasons beginning in 1989. He ran for more than 1,000 yards every year and still was at the top of his game when he retired.

11

GREEN BAY PACKERS

Scott Wells (63) and Aaron Rodgers (12)

There's a reason that football folks call Green Bay "Titletown." The Packers, who joined the NFL in the league's second season (1921), have won more championships than any other team. Green Bay won the first two Super Bowls (in the 1966 and 1967 seasons), plus Super Bowl XXXI (1996 season) and Super Bowl XLV (2010 season). Before the Super Bowl began, they won nine NFL titles. In all, that's a total of 13 league championships.

Green Bay's history is filled with some of the most famous names in football. In the 1930s and 1940s, Don Hutson was the NFL's first great pass catcher. In the 1960s, linebacker Ray Nitschke keyed a defense that helped the Packers win five championships in a span of seven seasons under legendary coach Vince Lombardi. In the 1990s, quarterback Brett Favre launched a career that eventually made him the NFL's all-time leading passer.

The team's glory days aren't just in the past, however. In the 2010 season, the Packers made the playoffs for the seventh time since the decade of the 2000s began. They were a wild-card team that had a tough road to get to the Super Bowl: three games away from home. They won all three, though, then beat the Pittsburgh Steelers 31-25 in Super Bowl XLV.

John Kuhn

Today's Stars

Aaron Rodgers is the latest in a long line of great Packers' quarterbacks. Since becoming a starter in the 2008 season, he's averaged 4,131 yards and 29 touchdown passes a season. His big-play wide receiver is Greg Jennings, who has a real nose for the end zone. On defense, linebacker Clay Matthews has made the Pro Bowl in each of his first two NFL seasons beginning in 2009.

MINNESOTA VIKINGS

The history of the Minnesota Vikings has been a roller coaster. No other franchise in the NFL has been as consistently good while at the same time failing to achieve the ultimate goal: a Super Bowl championship.

Minnesota was an NFL expansion team — a new team added to the league — in 1961. After a few years of struggle, the Vikings became really good for a really long time. In the 13 seasons from 1968 to 1980, they finished in first place in their division 11 times. They made the Super Bowl in the 1969, 1973, 1974, and 1976 seasons. Each time, though, they lost.

Recent history has been more of the same: good but not quite good enough. In 1998, the Vikings had the NFL's highest-scoring team ever and lost only one game in the regular season, but then lost in the playoffs. In 2009, another high-scoring team missed going to the Super Bowl when the Saints kicked a field goal in overtime at the conference championship game. In 2010, Minnesota was picked by many experts to win it all, but fell far back in the pack. This year, Vikings' fans hope their roller-coaster ride takes them back to the playoffs.

Adrian Peterson

Today's Stars

Offensive linemen don't get noticed much, but the Vikings have a lineman you can't miss in 6-foot 5-inch, 313-pound guard Steve Hutchinson. He's made the Pro Bowl seven times in his 10 NFL seasons, and he's helped running back Adrian Peterson post some amazing numbers early in his career. When the Vikings want to pass, young wideouts Sidney Rice and Percy Harvin are capable of making big plays.

Steve Hutchinson

Purple People Eaters

The Vikings' teams of the late 1960s and the early 1970s featured some of the NFL's best defenses ever — and one of its best nicknames ever, too! The defensive line on those teams was known as the Purple People Eaters. The name came from a No. 1 song from the late 1950s. The defensive ends on the Vikings' line were Carl Eller and Jim Marshall. The defensive tackles were Gary Larsen and Alan Page.

NFC South

The teams of the NFC South are the new kids on the block. Each of these four teams — the Atlanta Falcons, Carolina Panthers, New Orleans Saints, and Tampa Bay Buccaneers — began as an NFL expansion team.

Because the NFC South did not exist before 2002, its four teams all migrated from other divisions. The Falcons, Panthers, and Saints all played in the NFC West from the first year of that division in 1970 through 2001. The Buccaneers played their first season (1976) in the AFC West, then moved to the NFC Central through 2001.

Since the NFC South was created, no other division in the league has been quite as topsy-turvy. In 2002, for instance, Tampa Bay won the division and Carolina finished in last place. The next year, Carolina finished in first place and Atlanta in last place. Naturally, Atlanta won the division in 2004. That pattern continued until Carolina broke the string in 2008. The Panthers won the division after finishing in second place in 2007. In 2008, the Falcons came in second place and earned a wild-card playoff berth after *they* finished in last place in 2007.

All of that, of course, is good news for Carolina in 2011 — the Panthers finished in last place in the division in 2010!

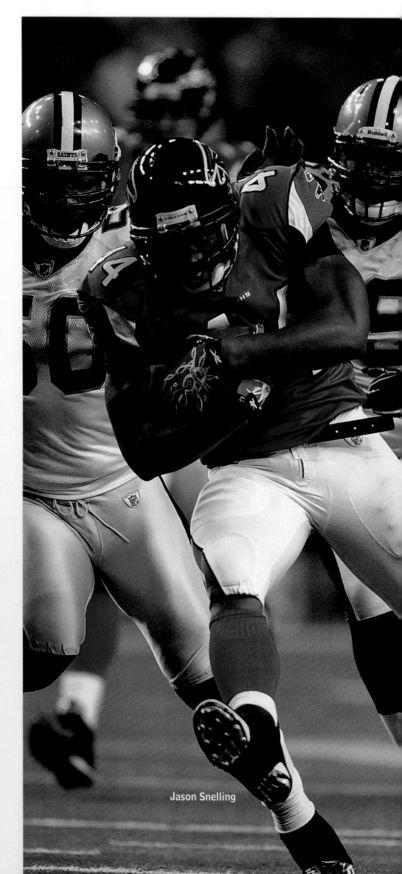

Jason Snelling

ATLANTA FALCONS

Since the late 1990s, the Atlanta Falcons have taken dizzying trips from near the top of the NFL, to near the bottom, and back near the top again. These days, they are near the top . . . and the Falcons hope they can stay and enjoy the view there for a little while!

The Falcons' franchise began in 1966. Atlanta drafted a great quarterback in Steve Bartkowski in 1975 and a great running back in William Andrews in 1979, but the team reached the playoffs only five times before 1998. Then everything changed. In the 1998 season, under veteran NFL coach Dan Reeves, the Falcons won a club-record 14 regular-season games and reached the Super Bowl for the first time. (They lost to the Denver Broncos.)

Since then, it's been an up-and-down ride. The year after going to the Super Bowl, the Falcons won only five games. In 2008, new coach Mike Smith took over a team that won only four games the year before. But the Falcons went 11-5 in 2008 and made the playoffs. The team missed the playoffs in 2009, then rebounded to win 13 games and the NFC South in 2010.

Matt Ryan

Today's Stars

Quarterback Matt Ryan is known for being cool under pressure. Ryan's favorite target is wide receiver Roddy White, who led the NFL with a Falcons-record 115 catches in 2010 and made the Pro Bowl for the third year in a row. In all, nine Falcons — the most in the NFL — made the Pro Bowl that season.

Roddy White

15

CAROLINA PANTHERS

The Carolina Panthers didn't take long to make their mark in the NFL. In 1995, in just the ninth game the Panthers ever played, Carolina stunned the San Francisco 49ers — who won Super Bowl XXIX in the 1994 season — 13-7. What's the big deal? Well, no expansion team ever had beaten a reigning Super Bowl champion before.

By that time, though, it already was apparent that the Panthers were no ordinary expansion team. Expansion teams usually are lucky to win a few games their first season. The Panthers won seven! The next year, Carolina was in the playoffs. By their ninth season, in 2004, they were in the Super Bowl. (They lost a close game to the New England Patriots.)

Almost from the start, the Panthers' formula has been to run the ball and play strong defense. When Carolina does have to pass, it can rely on big-play wide receiver Steve Smith. One of the best NFL players ever at gaining yards after the catch, Smith is the franchise's all-time receiving leader.

Not even Smith, though, could save Carolina in 2010. Without a proven quarterback, and with injuries hitting several key positions, the Panthers faltered badly last year. Carolina won only two games. After nine seasons, head coach John Fox was let go. Former NFL linebacker Ron Rivera was hired to turn things around in 2011.

Jonathan Stewart

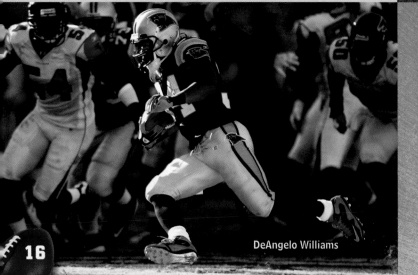

DeAngelo Williams

Today's Stars

It was a rough year all around for the Panthers in 2010, but new head coach Ron Rivera has some talent to work with. Up front, Pro Bowl offensive linemen Ryan Kalil and Jordan Gross block for running backs Jonathan Stewart and DeAngelo Williams. On defense, all-star linebacker Jon Beason is a tackling machine.

NEW ORLEANS SAINTS

It took a long time for the New Orleans Saints to become a winning team. When they won 11 games in 2010, it marked the eighth time since the 2000s began that they won at least as many games as they lost.

The Saints' franchise dates to 1966. (It officially was founded on All Saints' Day, of course!) But for the first 20 years of their existence, the Saints never won more games than they lost in a season. Things got so bad that fans took to calling them the "Aints." But then everything started to change after Louisiana native Bobby Hebert took over at quarterback. He led the team to the playoffs four times in six seasons beginning in 1987.

Still, the team's greatest success didn't come until quarterback Drew Brees and head coach Sean Payton arrived together in 2006. That year, the Saints won 10 games and their first NFC South championship. Three years later, New Orleans won the Super Bowl.

Drew Brees

Super Saints

The city of New Orleans was still rebuilding from 2005's Hurricane Katrina when the Saints gave the entire region a reason to cheer in the 2009 season. New Orleans, which has hosted the Super Bowl more times than any other city except Miami, had never sent its own team to the Big Game. But that year, the Saints rode a powerful offense to 13 wins in a row to start the season, and then to victory over the Colts in Super Bowl XLIV.

Sean Payton

Today's Stars

The Saints are loaded with good players, but the team's success revolves around its biggest star: quarterback Drew Brees. In five years in New Orleans, Brees has posted some amazing passing stats. On defense, linebacker Jonathan Vilma made the Pro Bowl in both the 2009 and 2010 seasons.

TAMPA BAY BUCCANEERS

The Tampa Bay Buccaneers raised the Vince Lombardi Trophy as Super Bowl champions in 2002, the 27th season of their existence. It was hard to believe it was the same franchise that lost every game it played its first season.

Tampa Bay's 0-14 record in 1976 was the worst of it, but the Buccaneers posted only three winning records before 1997. Then the team started winning regularly. With star players such as linebacker Derrick Brooks, Tampa Bay featured a quick and powerful defense that specialized in taking away the ball from its opponents. Everything came together in the 2002 season, when the Buccaneers won a club-record 12 games during the regular season, then won the Super Bowl.

After posting winning records six times in the first nine seasons of the 2000s, the Buccaneers suddenly found themselves in rebuilding mode in 2009. The superstars on defense were getting older or switching to other teams. Tampa Bay won only three games under first-year coach Raheem Morris. But in 2010, the Buccaneers surprised everyone by winning 10 games. The journey to the top had begun again — and the Buccaneers are certain the trip will be a lot quicker this time!

Josh Freeman

Trading Places

In 2002, the Buccaneers made a very unusual trade: They traded for a head coach! That's right — Tampa Bay sent two first-round draft picks, two second-round draft picks, and $8 million in cash to the Oakland Raiders. In return, the Raiders sent the Buccaneers their head coach, Jon Gruden. That was a very steep price. But in his first season in Tampa Bay, Gruden led the Buccaneers to the NFL championship. What team did they beat 48-21 in Super Bowl XXXVII? The Raiders, the team that traded Gruden!

Today's Stars

The Buccaneers fielded the youngest team in the NFL in 2010. The heart and soul of the team, though, is 15-year veteran Ronde Barber. The star cornerback is the franchise's all-time leader with 40 career pass interceptions. On offense, the Buccaneers have put their faith in young quarterback Josh Freeman.

For many years, this division has been known as the Wild, Wild West. The Arizona Cardinals, St. Louis Rams, San Francisco 49ers, and Seattle Seahawks have featured entertaining, high-scoring offenses that have produced a whole lot of victories — and several championships, too.

The NFC West has existed since the 1970 season, but it has had a few different looks over the years which have featured the Atlanta Falcons, New Orleans Saints, and the Carolina Panthers. Only the 49ers and Rams have been in the division since the beginning.

In 1976, the Seahawks played for just one season in the NFC West before moving to the AFC. In 2002 the NFC West welcomed back the Seahawks and added the Arizona Cardinals. And that's where we are today.

In the nine seasons since the current makeup of the NFC West, every team has had a turn at the top. In 2010, the championship came down to the last game of the season, when the Seahawks beat the Rams in a winner-take-all game for the title.

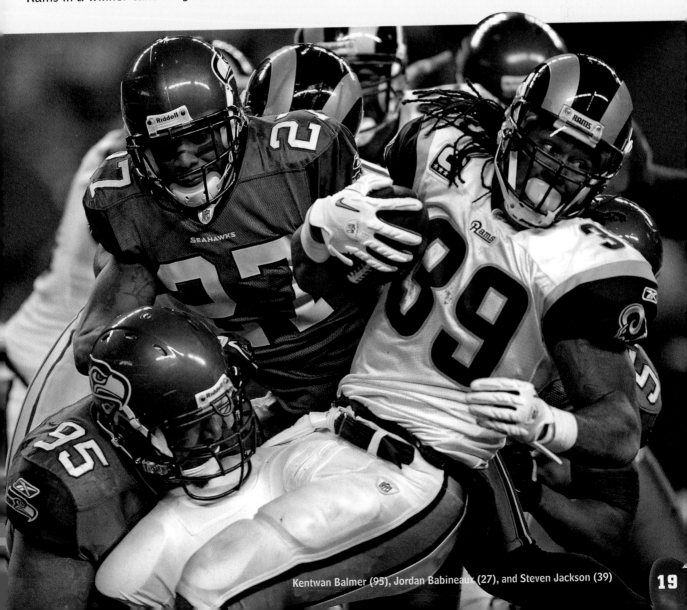

Kentwan Balmer (95), Jordan Babineaux (27), and Steven Jackson (39)

ARIZONA CARDINALS

The Cardinals are the oldest franchise in pro football. When the Cardinals first took the field as a neighborhood team in Chicago in 1898 William McKinley was the President of the United States.

When the NFL began in 1920, the team was based in Chicago and called the Racine Cardinals. They became the Chicago Cardinals in 1922, the St. Louis Cardinals in 1960, the Phoenix Cardinals in 1988, and the Arizona Cardinals in 1994.

Even though the Cardinals have been around for more than 100 years, their best days have come recently. The team did win NFL titles in 1925 and 1947, but then didn't win another postseason game until 1998. In 2005, Super Bowl-winning quarterback Kurt Warner joined the team. In 2008, Warner passed for a club-record 30 touchdowns to lead the Cardinals to their first NFC West championship. The Cardinals won the NFC title and lost to the Steelers in the Super Bowl on a last-minute touchdown.

The Cardinals won the NFC West again in 2009, but then Warner retired. In 2010, the team slumped to only five victories.

Larry Fitzgera

Adrian Wilson

Today's Stars

Just three years after playing in the Super Bowl, th Cardinals find themselves rebuilding for the future But two players from that NFC championship tear give them great building blocks. On offense, it' dynamic wide receiver Larry Fitzgerald. He's caugh more than 90 passes for more than 1,000 yards fou years in a row. On defense, veteran Adrian Wilson i a big-play safety.

Sam Bradford

The Rams' franchise is a tale of three cities. The team began as the Cleveland Rams in 1937, moved to Los Angeles in 1946, and has played in its current home in St. Louis since 1995. But wherever the team has been based, it has won a championship thanks to a great offense.

With such all-time greats as quarterbacks Bob Waterfield, Norm Van Brocklin, and Kurt Warner, running backs Ollie Matson and Marshall Faulk, and wide receivers Elroy "Crazylegs" Hirsch and Isaac Bruce, it's little wonder the Rams always have put points on the scoreboard. In the late 1990s and early 2000s, the Rams' offense was nicknamed "The Greatest Show on Turf." St. Louis won Super Bowl XXXIV in the 1999 season.

It was shocking, then, when St. Louis tumbled to the bottom of the offensive rankings during the 2009 season in which it won only one game. But with new quarterback Sam Bradford leading the way, the team rebounded to win seven games in 2010 — and to show some of that old spark on offense!

Breaking the Color Barrier

In 1946 (one year before Jackie Robinson broke baseball's color barrier with the Brooklyn Dodgers), the Rams signed African-Americans Woody Strode and Kenny Washington. At the time, there were no African-Americans playing in the NFL. The same year, the Cleveland Browns, who played in the All-America Football Conference then, signed African-Americans Marion Motley and Bill Willis. Those four men together broke the color barrier in pro football.

Today's Stars

Quarterback Sam Bradford was the top pick of the NFL Draft in 2010. He had the best rookie season of any first-year quarterback since the Colts' Peyton Manning in 1998. Running back Steven Jackson made the Pro Bowl in the 2010 season for the third time. On defense, emerging star Chris Long (a defensive end) is the son of Pro Football Hall of Fame defensive end Howie Long.

SAN FRANCISCO 49ERS

When you talk about the history of the San Francisco 49ers, there's only one place to start: at quarterback. From Frankie Albert in the 1940s, to Y.A. Tittle in the 1950s, to John Brodie in the 1960s and 1970s, to Joe Montana in the 1980s, and to Steve Young in the 1990s, the franchise has featured some of the greatest quarterbacks in NFL history. Montana quarterbacked the 49ers to four Super Bowl victories in the 1980s; the team added another with Young at quarterback in the 1994 season.

Oh, yeah, there was a pretty good receiver in there, too. Jerry Rice, who played in San Francisco from 1985 to 2000, caught more passes for more yards and more touchdowns than anybody else who ever played the game.

Ironically, the 49ers' biggest current need is at quarterback. San Francisco has struggled in recent seasons while trying to find the right player at the position. After the 49ers slumped to only six wins in 2010, they hired former Stanford coach Jim Harbaugh. Harbaugh's first job will be to settle on a quarterback. He should have some insight — he was a former quarterback himself!

Jerry Rice

Today's Stars

Whoever ends up being the 49ers' quarterback in 2011 will have some talented players around him, like running back Frank Gore, tight end Vernon Davis, and wide receiver Michael Crabtree. The biggest 49ers' star, though, is on defense. He's Patrick Willis, a linebacker who has made the Pro Bowl each of his four seasons in the NFL.

The Catch

The start of the 49ers' great dynasty of the 1980s began with "The Catch." In the final minute of the 1981 NFC Championship Game between the 49ers and the Dallas Cowboys, wide receiver Dwight Clark leaped high in the air to make a fingertip touchdown catch and give San Francisco a 28-27 victory. It sent the 49ers to their first Super Bowl, where they beat the Cincinnati Bengals.

SEATTLE SEAHAWKS

Matt
Hasselbeck

Compared to the other teams in the NFC West, the Seahawks haven't been around very long. But since the division got its current four-team setup in 2002, Seattle has been the team to beat. The Seahawks have won the division five times in the last seven seasons, including 2010.

Seattle began as an NFL expansion team in 1976 and played in the NFC West that first season. But from 1977 to 2001, the team played in the AFC West. The Seahawks had only limited success in their AFC days, and made the playoffs only five times. Those years did produce the best player in franchise history, though: Wide receiver Steve Largent, who was inducted into the Pro Football Hall of Fame in 1995.

Under head coach Mike Holmgren, the Seahawks had their greatest success in the mid-2000s. In the 2005 season, they made it to the Super Bowl for the first time, but lost to the Steelers. In 2010, Pete Carroll took over as coach and led Seattle to the NFC West title despite only seven wins. Still, the Seahawks proved they belonged in the playoffs when they upset defending Super Bowl-champion New Orleans 41-36 in the opening round.

Today's Stars

Seattle is a team of fresh faces — more than half of the players in 2010 were new to the team that season. One player among the holdovers from 2009 was quarterback Matt Hasselbeck, who is the team's all-time leader in passing yards. He figures to be pushed for playing time, though, by young Charlie Whitehurst. On defense, linebacker Lofa Tatupu is the Seahawks' player who almost always is around the ball.

Lofa Tatupu

NFC Standings

2010 NFC Standings:

NFC East	W	L	Pct.
Philadelphia	10	6	.625
New York Giants	10	6	.625
Dallas	6	10	.375
Washington	6	10	.375

NFC South	W	L	Pct.
Atlanta	13	3	.812
New Orleans	11	5	.688
Tampa Bay	10	6	.625
Carolina	2	14	.125

NFC North	W	L	Pct.
Chicago	11	5	.688
Green Bay	10	6	.625
Detroit	6	10	.375
Minnesota	6	10	.375

NFC West	W	L	Pct.
Seattle	7	9	.438
St. Louis	7	9	.438
San Francisco	6	10	.375
Arizona	5	11	.312

Postseason Results:

(Home team in ALL CAPS.)

NFC Wild-Card Playoff Games

SEATTLE 41, New Orleans 36

Green Bay 21, PHILADELPHIA 16

NFC Divisional Playoff Games

Green Bay 48, ATLANTA 21

CHICAGO 35, Seattle 24

NFC Championship Game

Green Bay 21, CHICAGO 14

Super Bowl XLV

Green Bay 31, Pittsburgh 25

at Cowboys Stadium, North Texas

SCHOLASTIC INC.

NEW YORK   TORONTO   LONDON   AUCKLAND
SYDNEY   MEXICO CITY   NEW DELHI   HONG KONG

Photo Credits

Page 4: © Winslow Townson/Associated Press; Page 5: © Mike Groll/Associated Press; Page 6: (top) © David Stluka/Associated Press, (bottom) © Lynn Sladky/Associated Press; Page 7: (left) © Charles Krupa/Associated Press, (right) © Windslow Townson/Associated Press; Page 8: (top) © Tony Dejak/Associated Press, (bottom) © Kathy Willens/Associated Press; Page 9: © David Drapkin/Associated Press; Page 10: (top) © Jeff Roberson/Associated Press, (bottom) © Ben Leibenberg/Associated Press; Page 11: (top) © Associated Press, (bottom) © Gail Burton/Associated Press; Page 12: (top) © Gene J. Puskar/Associated Press, (bottom) © Mark Duncan/Associated Press; Page 13: (top) © Gene J. Puskar/Associated Press, (bottom) © Harry Cabluck/Associated Press; Page 14: © AJ Mast/Associated Press; Page 15: (top) © Donna McWilliam/Associated Press, (bottom) © Bill Baptist/Associated Press; Page 16: (top) © AJ Mast/Associated Press, (bottom) © NFL/Associated Press; Page 17: (top) © Bill Baptist/Associated Press, (bottom) © Scott A. Miller/Associated Press; Page 18: (top) © Tom DiPace/Associated Press; (bottom) © Frederick Breedon/Associated Press; Page 19: © Bill Nichols/Associated Press; Page 20: (top) © Bill Nichols/Associated Press, (bottom) © NFL/Associated Press; Page 21: (top) © Reed Hoffmann/Associated Press, (bottom) © Charlie Riedel/Associated Press; Page 22: (top) © Greg Trott/Associated Press, (bottom) © Ben Margot/Associated Press; Page 23: Kevin Terrell/Associated Press

Design Elements

Starburst © Maliketh/iStockphoto; Football © Cscredon/iStockphoto; Yardage markers © Liewluck/Shutterstock

ISBN 978-0-545-34637-5

12 11 10 9 8 7 6 5 4 3 2 1   11 12 13 14 15/0

Cover design by Cheung Tai / Interior design by Rocco Melillo

Printed in the U.S.A.

First printing, September 2011

When the American Football League (AFL) began in the 1960 season, the idea of competing for players and fans with the established National Football League (NFL) was preposterous. Few people believed this new league would make it, which is why the owners of the eight original AFL franchises were called the "Foolish Club."

Well, it turns out those owners weren't so foolish after all. Not only did the AFL make it, but after gaining two additional teams, the league eventually merged with the NFL. Beginning in 1970, the post-merger NFL was split into the American Football Conference (AFC) and the National Football Conference (NFC). The teams in the AFC were the former AFL teams.

But there was one problem: There were 16 teams in the NFL and only 10 in the AFL. To even things out, the NFL had to convince three of its teams to switch sides. That wasn't very easy because NFL teams considered the AFL an inferior league. In the end, the Baltimore (now Indianapolis) Colts, Cleveland Browns, and Pittsburgh Steelers joined the AFC.

The Miami Dolphins, Oakland Raiders, and Pittsburgh Steelers dominated the AFC in the 1970s. Those teams also dominated their NFC foes in the Super Bowl. Then, after a lengthy dry spell for AFC teams, the Denver Broncos won the Super Bowl in the 1997 and 1998 seasons. The New England Patriots had a big stretch in the early 2000s, winning the Super Bowl three times.

The Steelers made it to their record-tying eighth Super Bowl in the 2010 season but lost to the NFC's Green Bay Packers. Still, with six victories, Pittsburgh has won the Super Bowl more times than any other team. In all, nine of the sixteen AFC teams have won the Super Bowl. Cleveland, Houston, and Jacksonville are the only AFC teams that have never made it to the big game.

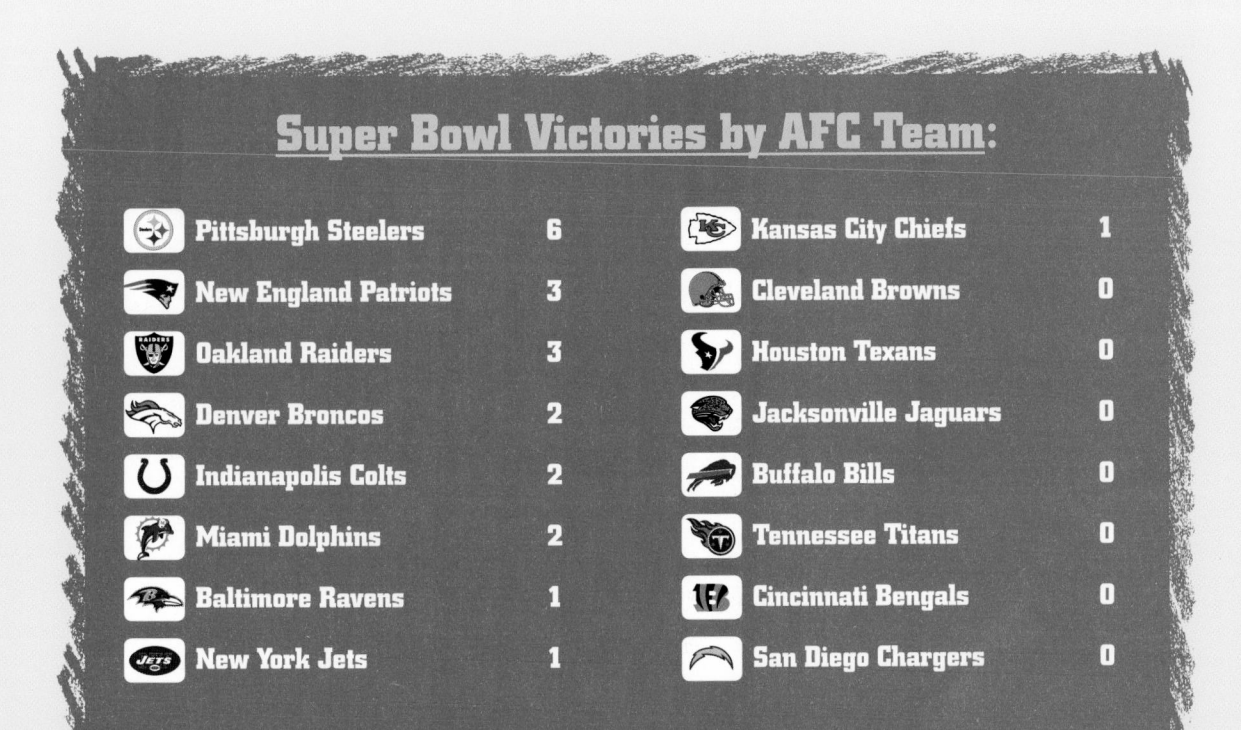

Super Bowl Victories by AFC Team:

Team	Wins	Team	Wins
Pittsburgh Steelers	6	Kansas City Chiefs	1
New England Patriots	3	Cleveland Browns	0
Oakland Raiders	3	Houston Texans	0
Denver Broncos	2	Jacksonville Jaguars	0
Indianapolis Colts	2	Buffalo Bills	0
Miami Dolphins	2	Tennessee Titans	0
Baltimore Ravens	1	Cincinnati Bengals	0
New York Jets	1	San Diego Chargers	0

Three of the original "Foolish Club" franchises from the AFL — the Buffalo Bills, New England Patriots, and New York Jets — are among the four teams in the AFC East. The fourth team, the Miami Dolphins, joined the AFL as an expansion team (a team added to an existing league) in 1966.

The AFC East was formed when the post-merger NFL was split into the American Football Conference (AFC) and the National Football Conference (NFC). The Colts were placed in the AFC East along with the Bills, Patriots (who were called the Boston Patriots at the time), Dolphins, and Jets. The division remained unchanged until the Colts were placed in the newly created AFC South for the 2002 season.

The Jets won the first four-team AFC East championship in the 2002 season, but the division has pretty much belonged to the New England Patriots ever since. The NFL's best team of the opening decade of the 2000s, New England won the first of five division championships in a row in 2003. After the Dolphins had a turn in 2008, the Patriots were back on top in both 2009 and 2010.

Tom Brady

BUFFALO BILLS

C.J. Spiller

Buffalo Bills fans have experienced a wide range of emotions while rooting for their team. They know the joy of a winning stretch, but also the disappointment of coming *this close* to winning it all, only to fall short. And that was just in one span of several seasons in the early 1990s!

In 1990, with Hall of Fame quarterback Jim Kelly directing a fast-paced offense, the Bills piled up the most points in the league on their way to the Super Bowl for the first time. They had a chance to beat the New York Giants in Super Bowl XXV that season, but a long field-goal try on the last play just missed. Buffalo returned to the Super Bowl the next season, but lost again…and then again the next season…and again the season after that! No other team ever has played in four Super Bowls in a row. Of course, no other team has lost four in a row, either.

Since their Super Bowl run in the 1990s, they've struggled to get back near the top. Buffalo won only four games in 2010 and is still looking for its first trip to the playoffs since the 2000s began.

Today's Stars

The Bills hope that dynamic running back C.J. Spiller, a first-round draft pick in 2010, can bring some explosiveness to their offense. He teams with Fred Jackson, who is an excellent pass-catcher as well as a runner. Kyle Williams anchors the defense from the interior of the Bills' line. He had his best season in 2010, when he made the Pro Bowl for the first time.

Kyle Williams

Comeback Kids

In the 1992 playoffs, the Bills pulled off one of the greatest comebacks in NFL history. Fans in Buffalo were already heading to the parking lots after their team fell behind the Houston Oilers 35-3 in the third quarter. A win seemed impossible, but Buffalo tied the game at 38-38, and then won 41-38 in overtime.

MIAMI DOLPHINS

The Miami Dolphins will always hold a unique place in NFL history. In 1972, Miami became the first (and, so far, only) team to complete a perfect season. That year, the Dolphins won all 17 regular season and postseason games, and finished with a 14-7 victory over the Washington Redskins in Super Bowl VII. This feat will never be exactly beaten since the NFL went from 17 to 19 total scheduled games in a season in 1978.

That's the biggest highlight in the Dolphins' history, but it is hardly the only one. The team came a long way in a short time after joining the AFL as an expansion team in 1966. Between 1971 and 1973, the Dolphins became the first team to play in three Super Bowls in a row. They won Game VIII in the 1973 season to become the second team to win back-to-back Super Bowls. Head coach Don Shula won more games than any other head coach in NFL history. In 1984, quarterback Dan Marino took Miami to the Super Bowl when he became the first player to pass for more than 5,000 yards in a season. (They lost to the 49ers.)

Marino retired following the 1999 season, and the 2000s have not been as kind to the Dolphins. The low point came in the 2007 season, when the team won only one game. In 2008, though, the Dolphins improved, winning 11 games and the Eastern Division title under first-year coach Tony Sparano. Miami was 7-9 and missed the playoffs in both 2009 and 2010.

Dan Marino

Today's Stars

The Dolphins chose Jake Long, an athletic and hulking (6-foot 7-inch, 317-pound) tackle from Michigan with the top pick of the 2008 NFL Draft. Long has played every game since and made the Pro Bowl each year. Another star is wide receiver Brandon Marshall who arrived via trade with Denver in 2010. Marshall caught 86 passes his first season in Miami.

Brandon Marshall

NEW ENGLAND PATRIOTS

The NFL's Super Bowl dynasties are pretty well defined. In the 1960s, the dynasty was the Green Bay Packers. In the 1970s, it was the Pittsburgh Steelers followed by the San Francisco 49ers in the 1980s, and the Dallas Cowboys in the 1990s. The opening decade of the 2000s belonged to the New England Patriots.

That Super Bowl run could not come soon enough. The team began as the Boston Patriots in the AFL in 1960. (The Patriots got the New England name in 1971.) For the franchise's first 40 seasons, the team's record was mixed. The 1985 squad made it to Super Bowl XX, but was routed by the Bears in that game.

Then, in 2000, Bill Belichick was hired as coach, and the Patriots drafted quarterback Tom Brady. Belichick's first team won only five games, but the Patriots have won more games than they lost every season since. Brady took over as the starter in 2001, and the team won the Super Bowl for the first of three times in four seasons. In 2007, the Patriots became the first team to win every regular-season game since the NFL went to a 16-game schedule in 1978, although they were upset by the Giants in the Super Bowl. In 2010, the Patriots went 14-2 and won the AFC East for the seventh time in eight seasons.

Tom Brady

Today's Stars

Quarterback Tom Brady is one of the NFL's marquee stars. He's protected by star linemen up front such as tackle Matt Light and guard Logan Mankins. Brady's top target is Pro Bowl receiver Wes Welker. But while the Patriots have been known mostly for their offense, they've taken steps to revitalize an aging defense, too, with young stars such as linebacker Jerod Mayo and safety Brandon Meriweather.

Jerod Mayo

NEW YORK JETS

The signature moment in the history of the New York Jets' franchise is easy to pinpoint. It came in the 1968 season, after the team won the AFL championship. The Jets played the NFL-champion Baltimore Colts in Super Bowl III. The mighty Colts had won 13 of 14 games and were favored to win by almost 20 points. And indeed, the game was no contest — but it was the Jets who won easily. New York took a shocking 16-0 lead and won 16-7.

Ever since, the Jets have had some pretty good years, especially in the 1980s. That was when the "New York Sack Exchange" defensive line helped the team reach the playoffs four times in six seasons beginning in 1981. But the team hasn't been back to the Super Bowl.

The current Jets' team is hopeful that they can break that drought. Under Rex Ryan, who became the head coach in 2009, the team has made the playoffs in back-to-back seasons. Along the way, they've rubbed some opposing teams and fans the wrong way, but their attitude carried them to the AFC Championship Game each of those years.

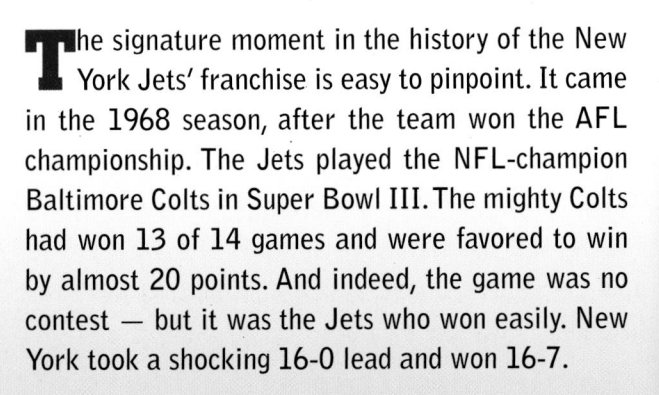

Mark Sanchez

Broadway Joe's Guarantee

As brash as the current Jets are, they've got nothing on Broadway Joe Namath, the quarterback who boldly guaranteed his team's shocking upset of the Colts in Super Bowl III a few days before the game. People scoffed at the notion of the Jets' winning— but Namath had the last laugh!

Darrelle Revis

Today's Stars

Cornerbacks aren't often game-changers, but the Jets' Darrelle Revis sure is. He always covers the opponents' best receiver — and almost always shuts him down! On offense, young Mark Sanchez has taken the Jets to back-to-back AFC title games.

Professional football traces its roots to the northeastern United States, where teams from Ohio and Pennsylvania played a rugged game in the early 1900s. That is still the preferred style of play in the AFC North. Two of the teams, the Cincinnati Bengals and the Cleveland Browns, are based in Ohio. The Baltimore Ravens play in Maryland but can trace their roots to Cleveland. And the Pittsburgh Steelers are from Pennsylvania. The AFC North was formed in 2002, when the NFL reassigned these four teams from the AFC Central Division.

Pittsburgh annually seems to be the team to beat in the AFC North. The Steelers won the first AFC North championship in 2002, and they have won the title four more times since then. The Ravens and Bengals each have won the division twice.

In 2010, the Steelers and Ravens both won 12 regular-season games. The teams split a pair of tough, low-scoring games against each other, but the division title went to the Steelers on a tiebreaker. Pittsburgh went on to win the AFC championship before losing an exciting game to the Green Bay Packers in the Super Bowl.

The Bengals had a down year in 2010 after finishing in first place in 2009. They hope to rebound to the top. And while the Browns have yet to win the AFC North, their solid corps of young players and a new coach for 2011 have their fans confident that a division title is coming soon.

BALTIMORE RAVENS

For a long time now, it's been all about defense with the Baltimore Ravens. But now the team has built an offense that makes this team a serious Super Bowl contender.

The Ravens have been in existence only since 1996. That was when the Cleveland Browns packed up and moved to Baltimore. Though most of the players were the same ones that played for the Browns the year before, the franchise was officially a brand-new team with a brand-new name.

After a couple of years in Baltimore, the Ravens won Super Bowl XXXV in 2000. They did it with a record-setting defense that shut down team after team. With linebacker Ray Lewis leading the way, the Ravens allowed opposing teams to score only 165 points all season — the lowest total ever allowed by an NFL team over a 16-game schedule. In the playoffs, Baltimore was even better. The Ravens outscored their four postseason opponents by a combined score of 95-23. They beat the New York Giants 34-7 in the Super Bowl. The Giants only points came on a kickoff return for a touchdown.

Since then, the Ravens have been to the playoffs six more times, but have missed the Super Bowl. Since 2008, the team has upgraded their offense with quarterback Joe Flacco, running back Ray Rice, and wide receiver Anquan Boldin. With that kind of offensive power, the rest of the NFL better be ready!

Joe Flacco

Ray Lewis

Today's Stars

In addition to Flacco, Rice, and Boldin, the Ravens have an impressive roster. Linebacker Ray Lewis made the Pro Bowl for the twelfth time in the 2010 season, and safety Ed Reed made it for the seventh time. But younger stars such as linebacker Terrell Suggs and lineman Haloti Ngata will be the ones carrying on the Ravens' defensive tradition.

CINCINNATI BENGALS

Paul Brown

When the Cincinnati Bengals began to play as an AFL expansion team in 1968, they had one big advantage over most expansion teams: Paul Brown. He was the team's founder, owner, general manager, and head coach — and he was inducted into the Pro Football Hall of Fame in 1967 for his work with the Cleveland Browns (the team that was named for him).

An innovative head coach, Brown got his new team up to speed pretty quickly. In 1970, they won the AFC Central Division championship. Brown went on to coach through the 1975 season. Though Cincinnati wasn't able to build on its early success, he left the team in good shape. By 1981, the Bengals won the AFC championship. They won it again in 1988. (Both times, they lost close games to the San Francisco 49ers in the Super Bowl.)

In the 1990s, the team had a long dry spell, but has had some very good years in the 2000s. In 2005, Cincinnati went 11-5 and won the AFC North for the first time. The Bengals won again with a 10-6 mark in 2009. In 2010, they slumped to only four victories. Still, they finished the season strong and hope to bounce back in 2011.

Worst to First

There is precedent for Bengals' fans to hope for a quick turnaround in 2011. Cincinnati has won seven division titles in its history. Four of those times, the Bengals won the division after finishing in last place the season before. So that's the bright side of the team's last-place finish in 2010!

Today's Stars

Quarterback Carson Palmer and wide receiver Chad Ochocinco have formed a formidable passing duo for several seasons now. But the Bengals have been most successful when they can run the ball behind workhorse Cedric Benson. He rushed for more than 1,000 yards for the Bengals in both 2009 and 2010.

Cedric Benson

CLEVELAND BROWNS

The history of the Cleveland Browns is really two different histories. The first is the history of the original Browns, who began play in the All-America Football Conference (AAFC) in 1946 and played in the NFL from 1950 to 1995. After that, the team moved to Baltimore and became the Ravens, leaving its logos, colors, and history behind.

The second history is when the new team began play in 1999. Even though it was considered a continuation of the original Browns' team, the second Browns' team was in reality starting from scratch. The original Browns' team went to 10 AAFC and NFL Championship Games in a row beginning in 1946. Cleveland won seven of those games (four in the AAFC and three in the NFL). The Browns featured lots of Hall of Famers such as quarterback Otto Graham, tackle Lou Groza, and coach Paul Brown. Later, another all-time great, Jim Brown, led Cleveland to the 1964 NFL title.

The new Browns won only two games in 1999 and three the next. The 2002 team earned a wild-card playoff berth, but then the team sunk to the bottom of the AFC North. In 2009, though, the team hired Mike Holmgren as its president and general manager. Holmgren, once a successful coach who took teams in Green Bay and Seattle to the Super Bowl, hired Pat Shurmur as the coach to restore Cleveland to its former glory.

Josh Cribbs

Dawg Pound

The three seasons without a football team (1996, 1997, and 1998) seemed like an eternity to Cleveland Browns fans — especially those with tickets in the Dawg Pound section of the stadium. These extreme fans long occupied a spot in the bleachers in the east end zone at Cleveland's Municipal Stadium, the original home of the team. That area was called the Dawg Pound. The team now plays at the new Cleveland Browns Stadium, but the Dawg Pound remains.

Today's Stars

The Browns have begun rebuilding behind a talented offensive line led by a pair of Pro Bowl players: center Alex Mack and tackle Joe Thomas. Quarterback Colt McCoy was a third-round draft pick in 2010 who had some impressive performances in his rookie season.

PITTSBURGH STEELERS

Steelers

Troy Polamalu

It took the Steelers more than 40 years to deliver a championship. Now the club seems to be making up for lost time. The Steelers have won the Super Bowl six times. That's more than any other team — and they narrowly missed a seventh championship in the 2010 season.

The team was known as the Pittsburgh Pirates when it began play in 1933. (Football teams back then sometimes took the same name as the baseball teams in their city.) In 1940, the team got its own name: the Steelers. The new identity didn't help much, though. The Steelers weren't very good for a long time.

That changed after Chuck Noll was hired as head coach. Noll drafted a bunch of great players, such as quarterback Terry Bradshaw, running back Franco Harris, linebacker Jack Lambert, and defensive tackle "Mean Joe" Greene. With the "Steel Curtain" defense leading the way, the Steelers won the Super Bowl in the 1974 and 1975 season. The offense played a bigger role when the team won again in the 1978 and 1979 seasons. The Steelers haven't won it all twice in a row since, but they have won in the 2005 and 2008 seasons. In 2010 they made it all the way to the Super Bowl before losing a narrow 31-25 decision to the Green Bay Packers.

Today's Stars

The Steelers roster is packed with stars. In 2010, safety Troy Polamalu was named the NFL's Defensive Player of the Year. Linebacker James Harrison won that same award two years earlier. Quarterback Ben Roethlisberger, running back Rashard Mendenhall, and wide receiver Mike Wallace are the playmakers on offense.

Miracle Catch

The Steelers pulled off perhaps the most famous play in NFL history. Pittsburgh was trailing the Raiders 7-6 and was down to its last chance in a 1972 playoff game: fourth-and-10 from its 40-yard line with 22 seconds left. Terry Bradshaw threw a long pass that was tipped away — but toward Steelers' running back Franco Harris. He grabbed the ball close to his shoetops and raced for the winning touchdown!

Franco Harris

13

Every good NFL team's roster includes a mix of talented veterans and rookies. Just like such a roster, the AFC South is a blend of franchises long established in the NFL and young teams still forging their identity.

The established teams are the Indianapolis Colts and the Tennessee Titans. The Colts have been around since 1953, although they originally played in Baltimore until moving to Indianapolis in 1984. The Titans have played since 1960, but they began their existence as the Houston Oilers. The team was still known as the Oilers for two years after moving to Tennessee before becoming the Titans in 1999.

The newer franchises are the Houston Texans and the Jacksonville Jaguars. The Texans are the NFL's youngest club. They began as an expansion team in 2002. The Jaguars aren't much older. They were an expansion team in 1995.

Only the Texans have spent their entire franchise life in the AFC South which was formed in 2002. In 1970, the Colts were placed in the AFC East, where they stayed through 2001.

In 2010, the Colts won the AFC South for the seventh time in the division's nine-year history. The only other team ever to win the division is Tennessee in 2002 and 2008. But fans in Houston and Jacksonville have reason to hope that their turn is coming soon.

Pierre Garcon (85) and Jason McCourty (30)

HOUSTON TEXANS

t Schaub

The fans in Houston have been crazy for their Texans ever since the franchise debuted as an NFL expansion team in the 2002 season. Now the Texans look like they might be on the verge of rewarding those loyal fans with a trip to the playoffs soon. A lot of folks figured that would have happened by now, especially when the Texans became the first team in 41 years to win their debut game. But things haven't gone quite as planned since then.

Under head coach Dom Capers and with David Carr (the top pick of the 2002 NFL Draft) at quarterback, the Texans gradually improved their second and third seasons. But then came the 2005 season and a major step back to only two victories. New head coach Gary Kubiak, a former NFL quarterback, came in 2006. The next year, Matt Schaub took over as quarterback. Again, the Texans gradually improved, until they posted their first winning record at 9-7 in 2009. But then came another step back to only six victories in the 2010 season.

So it's been two steps forward, one step back in this franchise's brief history. The Texans hope the next step forward takes them to the playoffs for the first time.

A Good Start!

body expects an expansion team beat one of the NFL's most storied anchises in its very first game. But at's just what the Texans did in 02. In its opening game, Houston ayed the Dallas Cowboys. The xans scored a touchdown the st time they had the ball and went to win 19-10.

Andre Johnson

Today's Stars

The Texans have built a dynamic passing game around quarterback Matt Schaub and wide receiver Andre Johnson. Schaub passed for more than 9,000 yards combined the last two seasons; Johnson has twice led the NFL in receiving. Now those players have been joined by a big-time running back, too. Arian Foster was the league's leading rusher in the 2010 season.

INDIANAPOLIS COLTS

The Colts have a long and illustrious history that includes many great players, great victories, and NFL championships. But there's no time quite like the present. The current Colts feature one of the greatest players in NFL history: quarterback Peyton Manning. And they have had a sustained run of success that took them to the playoffs in 2010 for the ninth season in a row. No NFL team ever has made it to the playoffs 10 years in a row.

The Colts began play in Baltimore in the 1953 season, and it didn't take them long to reach the top. In 1958, with Hall of Famer Johnny Unitas playing quarterback and end Gino Marchetti leading the defense, Baltimore won the first of back-to-back NFL championships. In 1970, the Colts joined the newly formed AFC and won the Super Bowl for the first time.

The Colts moved to Indianapolis in 1984, but didn't have much success until drafting Manning in 1998. The next year, they won 13 games and made the playoffs. The same season, Manning made the Pro Bowl for the first of 11 times in 12 years. The highlight came in 2006, when Indianapolis beat Chicago 29-17 in Super Bowl XLI.

Peyton
Manning

The Greatest Game Ever Played

The Colts (who were in Baltimore at the time) beat the New York Giants 23-17 in overtime to win the 1958 NFL championship in what is called The Greatest Game Ever Played. It got that lofty nickname because the drama kept a record television audience glued to its sets and raised pro football's stature on the national sports scene.

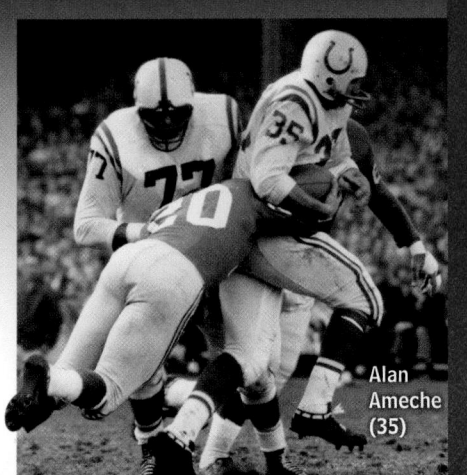

Alan
Ameche
(35)

Today's Stars

Quarterback Peyton Manning, who has started every game since he was drafted, has been the face of the Colts' franchise ever since the club selected him with the top pick of the 1998 draft. But the Colts couldn't have done it without other stars, too, such as wide receiver Reggie Wayne and defensive ends Dwight Freeney and Robert Mathis.

JACKSONVILLE JAGUARS

The Jaguars have only been around since 1995, when they entered the league as an expansion team. But they've already crammed a whole lot of history into their first 16 seasons.

Like the Carolina Panthers, Jacksonville's 1995 expansion counterparts in the NFC, the Jaguars were not a typical first-year team. Instead of struggling for a while, like expansion teams usually do, Jacksonville was already in the playoffs after going 9-7 in its second season.

That was a nice accomplishment, but even after the Jaguars earned a wild-card playoff berth that year, most football experts figured they would make a quick exit from the postseason. Instead, Jacksonville went on the road and shocked the powerful Buffalo Bills 30-27 in the opening round. Then the next week, they went to Denver and stunned the AFC West champs by the same score. Only a loss to the Patriots in the AFC title game kept them from the Super Bowl.

With Mark Brunell passing the ball, Fred Taylor rushing it, and Jimmy Smith catching it, the Jaguars built one of the best offenses in the NFL. They returned to the playoffs each of the next three seasons, including 1999, when they won a club-record 14 games. After a couple of down years, Jack Del Rio took over for Tom Coughlin as head coach in 2003. The Jaguars have returned to the playoffs twice more on Del Rio's watch, but are still looking for their first trip to the Super Bowl.

David Garrard

Today's Stars

The biggest star in Jacksonville is the smallest player on the roster. Maurice Jones-Drew is just 5 feet 7 inches, so there were a lot of questions when he came out of college about whether or not he could take the pounding that an NFL running back does. Well, the answers are in. Jones-Drew has averaged more than 1,000 rushing yards per season and has been a touchdown machine.

Maurice Jones-Drew

TENNESSEE TITANS

One of the original American Football League franchises in 1960, the Tennessee Titans began their existence as the Houston Oilers. The team moved to Tennessee in 1997 and kept the nickname Oilers at first; in 1999, they became known as the Titans.

The Oilers were the AFL's first great team. Behind quarterback and kicker George Blanda, who later would go on to even greater fame with the Raiders, Houston won each of the first two AFL titles. In the late 1960s, the Oilers became the first NFL team to play indoors, at the Houston Astrodome. Running back Earl Campbell carried the Oilers to the playoffs in the late 1970s, and head coach Jerry Glanville's intimidating defenses turned the Astrodome into the "House of Pain" for Oilers' opponents in the late 1980s.

With running back Eddie George and quarterback Steve McNair leading the way, the newly named Titans had several good teams in the late 1990s and early 2000s. The best was in 1999, when the team won 13 games and reached the Super Bowl before losing a close game to the Rams. Tennessee won the first AFC South title in 2002 and another crown in 2008 before slumping to only six wins in 2010.

Chris Johnson

Michael Griffin

Today's Stars

Titans running back Chris Johnson is one of the most exciting players in the NFL. He is a threat to score a touchdown anytime he touches the ball, whether rushing or receiving. In 2009, Johnson set an NFL record when he gained 2,509 yards from scrimmage (rushing yards plus receiving yards). Michael Griffin has become the star of the Titans' defense. The fourth-year safety made the Pro Bowl in the 2010 season.

The American Football League (AFL), which existed from 1960 to 1969, was a wild-and-crazy league that featured colorful characters and high-scoring football. The teams that best exemplified those traits have played together in the AFC West since the division was formed following the AFL-NFL merger in 1970.

The Denver Broncos, Kansas City Chiefs, Oakland Raiders, and San Diego Chargers made up a four-team AFC West until the expansion Tampa Bay Buccaneers joined them in 1976. The next year, the Buccaneers left and the Seattle Seahawks moved in until the 2001 season. In 2002, the division reverted to its original four-team format.

When these four teams were in the AFL, they always played in the same division, too. That means they've been playing each other twice every season — once at home and once on the road — for more than half a century now. This history makes their rivalries among the most intense in all of football!

The Raiders got the best of these rivalries in the 2010 season, when they won all six games against their division foes. Unfortunately, they didn't fare as well against the teams outside their division, and they missed the playoffs. The Chiefs did better against those other teams and won the AFC West despite losing twice to Oakland. The Chargers didn't make the playoffs last season, but they had a run of four consecutive AFC West titles from 2006 to 2009. And before that, it was the Broncos who ruled the division in 2005.

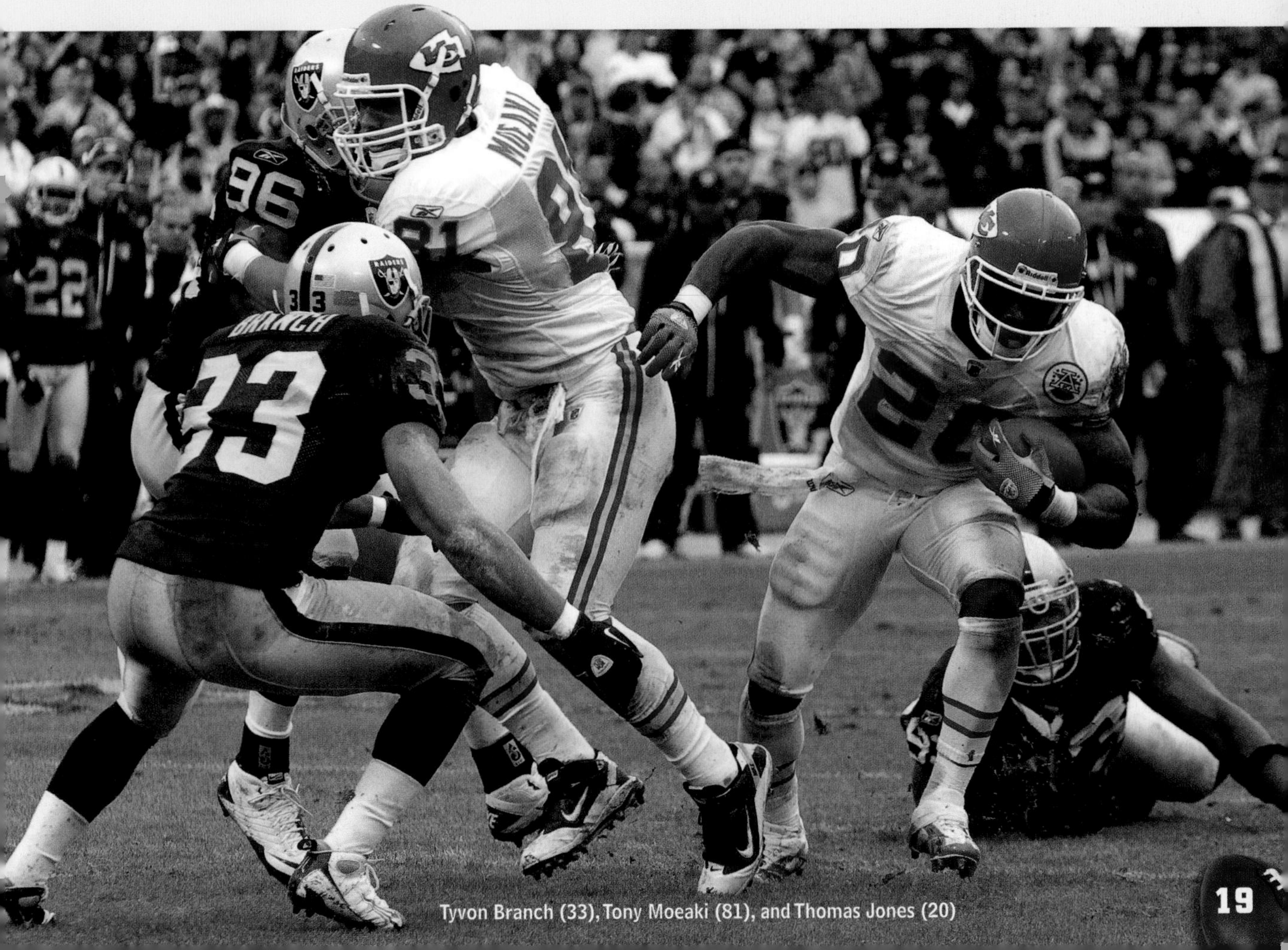

Tyvon Branch (33), Tony Moeaki (81), and Thomas Jones (20)

DENVER BRONCOS

The history of the Denver Broncos can be neatly summed up in three distinct time periods: Before John Elway, During John Elway, and After John Elway. During the Pro Football Hall of Fame quarterback's career (which lasted from 1983 to 1998), the Broncos had immense success. The Before and After parts? Not so much.

The Broncos were one of the AFL's charter franchises in 1960, but they averaged fewer than four wins per season in the league's 10 years. The Broncos didn't post a winning record, in fact, until 1977, when their famous "Orange Crush" defense took them to the Super Bowl. (They lost to Dallas.) After Elway arrived, though, he led the team to three Super Bowls in four seasons in the 1980s. Denver lost each time, but then broke through with back-to-back Super Bowl victories in Elway's final two NFL seasons.

In 2009, the team turned to Kyle Orton as the latest in a line of quarterbacks who have tried to fill Elway's big shoes. Orton posted decent statistics, but the team failed to post a winning record that season or the next. Instead, the Broncos' have high hopes for Tim Tebow, who was a first-round draft pick in 2010.

Champ Bailey

The 2000-Yard Man

The Broncos were really good, but not great, until they paired quarterback John Elway with running back Terrell Davis in 1995. Three years later, Davis had one of the greatest seasons of any running back in history: 2,008 rushing yards and 23 touchdowns scored. He is one of only six players ever to run for 2,000 yards in a single season.

Terrell Davis

Today's Stars

Veteran wideout Brandon Lloyd had a career-best season in 2010, when he led the NFL with 1,448 receiving yards. But the real players to watch are young quarterback Tim Tebow and running back Knowshon Moreno. They figure to be key cogs in helping Denver return to its winning ways. On defense, Champ Bailey is a shutdown cornerback who has been to the Pro Bowl 10 times in 12 NFL seasons.

KANSAS CITY CHIEFS

Football fans in general owe a debt of gratitude to the late Lamar Hunt, the man who owned the Chiefs' franchise until 2006. It was Hunt who was the driving influence behind the formation of the AFL.

In the late 1950s, Hunt tried to buy an NFL franchise to place in Dallas — before the Cowboys existed. When that failed, he started his own league! His team was the Dallas Texans. Though Dallas won the AFL championship in 1962, the team moved to Kansas City in 1963 after the Cowboys had been in Dallas for three years. In Kansas City, the franchise won league titles again in 1966 and 1969.

The AFL was generally considered inferior, but the Chiefs scored a victory for the AFL when they upset the NFL-champion Minnesota Vikings 23-7 in Super Bowl IV in the 1969 season. It was the last game ever played by an AFL team. The next year, the AFL teams joined the NFL as part of a merger agreement.

The Chiefs haven't won the Super Bowl since then, but they've had a lot of pretty good teams. Beginning in 1990, they made the playoffs six years in a row under head coach Marty Schottenheimer. And since the AFC West took its current shape in 2002, Kansas City has won the division twice. The most recent was in 2010. The Chiefs won 10 games that season after winning only four the year before.

Matt Cassel

Today's Stars

Head coach Todd Haley was the offensive coordinator of the Arizona Cardinals when they went to the Super Bowl in the 2008 season. Haley has helped turn around the Chiefs' offense with Matt Cassel at quarterback, Jamaal Charles at running back, and Dwayne Bowe at wide receiver. On defense, safety Eric Berry made the Pro Bowl in his rookie season in 2010.

Dwayne Bowe

OAKLAND RAIDERS

The Oakland Raiders have a long and proud heritage that began in the 1960 season when Oakland was one of the original AFL franchises. The Raiders had a slow start, but then they got really good for a long time. The team won the AFL championship in 1967, and then the Super Bowl in the 1976, 1980, and 1983 seasons. (This last victory came while the team played in Los Angeles from 1982 to 1994.) Along the way, the team featured some of pro football's best and most memorable characters, such as quarterback Ken "Snake" Stabler, linebacker Ted "The Mad Stork" Hendricks, and George Blanda, a quarterback and kicker who played until he was 48 years old in 1975.

In the early 2000s, the Raiders began a string of three years in a row in the playoffs, but they haven't been back since. Still, in 2010 the team won as many games as it lost for the first time since that stretch. The Raiders hope to feature a rejuvenated offense under coordinator Hue Jackson, who was promoted to head coach for 2011.

Darren McFadden

Today's Stars

The Raiders made an uncommon move when they drafted both a kicker, Sebastian Janikowski, and a punter, Shane Lechler, in 2000. But it worked out in their favor, because they've given Oakland a solid pair of specialists for more than a decade now. More recent draft picks such as running back Darren McFadden (in 2008) and wide receiver Jacoby Ford (in 2010) have helped fuel the offense.

Sebastian Janikowski (11) and Shane Lechler (9)

Name Games

The Raiders may have played in more famous games than any other team in NFL history. There was the Heidi Game against the Jets in 1968, the Immaculate Reception against the Steelers in 1972, the Sea of Hands against the Dolphins in 1974, the Ghost to the Post against the Colts in 1977, the Holy Roller against the Chargers in 1978, and the Tuck Rule Game against the Patriots in 2002. The Raiders won some and they lost some, but all of them were exciting!

SAN DIEGO CHARGERS

Philip Rivers

Over the years, the Chargers have featured a lot of good teams and great players. But this is one franchise for which the "good ol' days" might be right now. That's because the Chargers are in the midst of the longest prolonged period of success in their history. In 2010, San Diego finished at .500 or better (the Chargers were 9-7) for the seventh consecutive season.

The franchise began play as the Los Angeles Chargers in the first year of the American Football League in 1960. The next year, the team moved to San Diego. The Chargers played in 5 of the 10 title games in the AFL's existence and won the championship in 1963. The team also had a great run in the late 1970s and early 1980s, with Hall of Fame quarterback Dan Fouts throwing the ball in the "Air Coryell" offense (named for head coach Don Coryell). In 1994, the Chargers reached the Super Bowl for the first time, but were routed by the 49ers.

In 2006, young quarterback Philip Rivers took over as the starter and led the Chargers to a club-record 14 wins as San Diego made the playoffs for the first of four years in a row. In 2010, the Chargers won nine games but missed the playoffs. Still, they ranked among the NFL's best on both offense and defense. This is a team that looks like it might ready to put it all together for a run at the Super Bowl!

Today's Stars

True to their lineage, the current Chargers feature some of the NFL's top firepower. Quarterback Philip Rivers has passed for more than 4,000 yards three years in a row. Rivers throws to one of the best pass-catching tight ends in the NFL today in Antonio Gates. The Chargers also feature an up-and-coming star in running back Ryan Mathews.

Antonio Gates

AFC Standings

2010 AFC Standings:

AFC East	W	L	Pct.
New England	14	2	.875
New York Jets	11	5	.688
Miami	7	9	.438
Buffalo	4	12	.250

AFC South	W	L	Pct.
Indianapolis	10	6	.625
Jacksonville	8	8	.500
Houston	6	10	.375
Tennessee	6	10	.375

AFC North	W	L	Pct.
Pittsburgh	12	4	.750
Baltimore	12	4	.750
Cleveland	5	11	.313
Cincinnati	4	12	.250

AFC West	W	L	Pct.
Kansas City	10	6	.625
San Diego	9	7	.562
Oakland	8	8	.500
Denver	4	12	.250

Postseason Results:
(Home team in ALL CAPS.)

AFC Wild-Card Playoff Games
N.Y. Jets 17, INDIANAPOLIS 16

Baltimore 30, KANSAS CITY 7

AFC Divisional Playoff Games
PITTSBURGH 31, Baltimore 24

N.Y. Jets 28, NEW ENGLAND 21

AFC Championship Game
PITTSBURGH 24, N.Y. Jets 19

Super Bowl XLV
Green Bay 31, Pittsburgh 25

at Cowboys Stadium, North Texas